363.5

TALK ABOUT
Homelessness

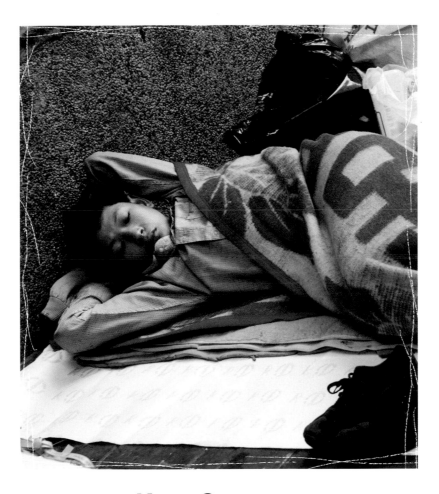

Kaye Stearman

WAYLAND

First published in 2008 by Wayland

Wayland
338 Euston Road
London NW1 3BH

Wayland Australia
Level 17/207 Kent Street
Sydney, NSW 2000

Editor: Camilla Lloyd
Consultant: Jayne Wright
Designer: Tim Mayer
Picture researcher: Kathy Lockley

Picture acknowledgments: The author and publisher would like to thank the following for allowing their pictures to be reproduced in this publication: Cover photograph: Peter Holmes/Photofusion Photo Library. Akhtar Soomro/epa/Corbis: 24; Alfredo Caliz/Panos Pictures: 23B; Alison Wright/Corbis: 14T, 21; Ashley Cooper/Corbis: 22TL, 29; Bob Sacha/Corbis: 31; Felix Heyder/DPA/PA Photos: 9; G.M.B. Akash/Panos Pictures: 12B, 13; Gerd Ludwig/Visum/Panos Pictures: 26-27; Giry Daniel/Corbis Sygma: 36T; Iain Masterton/Alamy: 35T; imagebroker/ Alamy: 17; Janine Wiedel Photolibrary/Alamy: 4, 20; Jim West/Alamy: 45; Joseph Sohm/Visions of America/Corbis: 42-43; Judith Wagner/ zefa/Corbis: 10TL bkg., 12-13T bkg., 14BR bkg., 18BL bkg., 22-23C bkg., 34, 35B bkg., 36BL bkg., 38 bkg.; Look Bildagentur der Fotografen GmbH/Alamy: 11; Mark Henley/Panos Pictures: 1, 8; Mark Peterson/ Corbis: 15; Mike Abrahams/Alamy: 18-19; Niall Carson/PA Archive/PA Photos: 39; PeerPoint/Alamy: 16; Peter Holmes/Photofusion Photo Library: 37; Robert van der Hilst/Corbis: 6-7; Sara Palazotti - www.sarapalazotti.com/Alamy: 30; Schiller Flemming/AP/PA Photos: 44; Shizuo Kambayashi/AP/PA Photos: 5; Stephen Finn/Alamy: 40; Sucheta Das/Reuters/Corbis: 42; SW Productions/Brand X/Corbis:41; vario images GmbH & Co.KG/Alamy: 10B; Viviane Moos/Corbis: 25, 28, 32-33.

Sources:
p.5 Japan Times Online, 29 August 2007.
p.7 West End Extra, UK, 20 July 2007.
p.7 source: Statistics derived from European Observatory on Homelessness, Fifth Review, 2006.
p.9 The Guardian, 23 July 2007.
p.12 The Guardian, 1 January 2004.
p.17 BBC News website, 29 November 2006.
p.41 US Government Figures, 2007.
p.27 Kleine Zeitung, Austria, 22 August 2007.
p.39 B. Ogdan, Austin, Texas in Timesonline, 20 July 2007.
p.43 Seattle Times, 12 June 2006.

British Library Cataloguing in Publication Data:
Stearman, Kaye
  Talk about homelessness
  1. Homelessness - Juvenile literature
  I. Title II. Homelessness
  362.5

ISBN: 978 0 7502 4934 8

Printed in China

Wayland is a division of Hachette Children's Books, an Hachette Livre UK Company
www.hachettelivre.co.uk

CONTENTS

Chapter 1
What is homelessness?

There are many different ways that people experience homelessness and no single description covers them all. The main types of homeless people are: roofless, homeless, hidden homeless and homeless at home.

Roofless people are homeless in the most basic sense, living and sleeping on the pavements, in doorways, railway and bus stations, in cars, even underground in the sewers. They are often referred to as street people, street sleepers or rough sleepers.

Homeless people live in temporary accommodation, including hostels or homeless shelters, hotels, bed and breakfasts (B&Bs) or flats with short leases of a few months, or they squat in empty or derelict buildings, with or without the owner's permission. The hidden homeless are those staying with friends and relatives, usually temporarily. Those who are homeless at home live in overcrowded or inadequate housing, sharing with others, sometimes for months or years.

Safe but not secure or comfortable, young homeless people find a temporary bed on someone else's floor. They are known as squatters or 'sofa surfers' (see page 19).

A billboard for a 24-hour Internet café in Japan. These Internet cafés offer a clean and safe place for thousands of homeless people who can't afford a room of their own.

People in the last two groups are often not recognized as homeless by government authorities and so are not allowed to apply for rehousing or financial support.

How many homeless people are there?

Attempts to count the numbers of homeless people run into many problems. Do we count just the people living on the streets or include people living in temporary accommodation? What about people moving between homes or waiting on a housing list? And do we include people living in unsatisfactory housing? Each time, the numbers get larger.

Two main counting methods are used. The first counts all the people who are homeless on a particular day or in a given week. The second method examines the number of homeless people over a longer period of time, such as a year. But many homeless people move from place to place, and in and out of different types of housing, so it is difficult to track them. For example, a person may move from sleeping on a friend's floor to a life on the streets, then into a hostel and then into temporary accommodation. It's easy to count the same person twice or three times, or not to count them at all.

In the media

Around 5,400 people with no fixed address spend their nights at 24-hour Internet cafés across Japan. Customers at a typical net café can stay overnight for ¥1,000 to ¥2,000 (¥1,000 is around £4) in a small cubicle equipped with a chair, computer and TV. Many cafés offer free soft drink refills and some even have showers.

On the streets

It might seem easy to count street people since they are often seen begging on the streets during the day or lying in office doorways at night, but it is difficult to estimate their numbers correctly. Many street people actively avoid figures of authority, such as police or social workers, fearing that they will be imprisoned or moved on. It is often said, that when a count is about to take place, the police move rough sleepers on to other areas.

In rich countries, rough sleepers are a small proportion of homeless people. There are many more people in temporary accommodation, or people who are 'hidden homeless'. Some of these people are included in government statistics, others are not.

The numbers of homeless people vary greatly between countries. The great majority of homeless people live in the cities of the developing world in Asia, Africa and Latin America. Richer countries have fewer homeless people than poorer ones. For example, in the UK there are half a million people registered as seeking permanent accommodation, plus others who do not register. In Australia, the 2000 census recorded 100,000 homeless people. In the USA, a recent estimate is that there are around 3.5 million homeless people, mainly women and young people.

Although life on the streets can be tough, some homeless people establish a permanent base on the pavement, like this woman in Buenos Aires, the capital city of Argentina.

It happened to me

'As a street sleeper myself, I can say that on numerous occasions street sleepers have been encouraged to be away from the area on the night of the count. Sometimes the police tell us not to be at our regular sleeping place. If they can't see us, it looks as though homelessness isn't a problem.'

Anonymous letter.

FACTS

NUMBER OF HOMELESS PEOPLE IN EUROPE

na = not available
Source: figures taken from *European Observatory on Homelessness, Fifth Review*, 2006.

COUNTRY	ROOFLESS	HOUSELESS	HIDDEN HOMELESS	HOMELESS AT HOME
Denmark	na	10,000	na	na
France	20,000	85,000	152,000	2,187,000
Germany	20,000	272,000	na	na
Ireland	500	600	3,000	6,000
Italy	30,000	na	na	23,500
Netherlands	3,000	10,000	na	na
Sweden	3,000	1,000	5,000	na
UK	2,000	112,000	na	3,000,000

Chapter 2

Why do people become homeless?

Homelessness can be explored in two different ways. Firstly, the housing situation as it affects society as a whole can be examined. Secondly, we can look at why particular individuals and groups are more at risk of becoming homeless than others.

The housing market affects society in a number of ways. It determines how many houses are available, their size and suitability, where they are located and how much they cost to buy or rent. If there is a general housing shortage, then rents go up and people must pay more for their housing. The richest people can afford the biggest homes in the best areas, while the poorest take the smallest places, share housing or move to areas where rents are lower. When the shortages are severe, the poorest people can become homeless.

A homeless teenager in China beds down on the street. He is just one of the millions of poor villagers who migrate to the cities in search of work.

Governments have built huge blocks of flats to house families. But high-rise flats are often unsuitable for young children. This photo shows government housing in Cologne, Germany.

Unsuitable housing

The issue of homelessness is very complex. There may be enough homes but they might not be in the right places. For example, there may be houses available in rundown or unsafe neighbourhoods, far from jobs, transport and other facilities. Other homes might not be suitable for families with young children; for example, small flats in high-rise blocks without play areas.

Owning a home

Most people want to buy their own home, but because it is expensive to do so they usually take out a mortgage – a long-term loan from the bank or building society. Mortgage-holders pay off the debt over many years. If interest rates rise, then most mortgage-holders must pay more towards the loan. Home ownership can bring security in the long term, so many people feel that mortgages are worthwhile. But not everyone wants, or can afford, to buy a house.

In the media

Nicole Goodwin fought in Iraq only to come back to New York to find herself homeless. She walked the streets for several weeks, from shelter to shelter, with her one-year-old child, Shylah, strapped to her chest and carrying their worldly possessions on her back and crammed into a pram.

Homes for rent

Many people rent houses, either from private landlords or in 'social housing' owned by government authorities or not-for-profit (charitable) organizations. In general, social housing costs less than renting from a private landlord, but is normally only available to the people who need it most, such as families with children or people with special needs (such as elderly or disabled people). People can spend a long time waiting for social housing, in the meantime renting privately or sharing with others.

In recent years, there has been extra pressure on housing, partly because of an expanding population and, in places, because of immigration. In the past, sharing rooms and facilities was commonplace, but today people want and expect better housing conditions. Families are also changing. More people live alone, and divorce and separation are more common, sometimes leading to a need for additional housing.

A family on the streets of New Delhi, India's capital. In India, cities are very crowded and many people are very poor. For some, life on the pavement is the only option.

Even in rich countries like Japan some people live on the streets. They are most likely to be men without jobs or family support and some are addicted to alcohol or drugs and have mental health problems.

Poverty and homelessness

Changes in the housing market may explain why there are shortages of housing and the problems this could cause. But they do not explain why some people become homeless or who is most at risk. To understand this we need to study individual circumstances. Every homeless person has his or her own story to tell. For some, being homeless is sudden and unexpected, for others it is a long, slow descent, and for a few it is a regular way of life.

DOs & DON'Ts

If you are thinking of running away from home read the action points below.

* Do talk over your thoughts and feelings with someone you trust and who can give advice.

* Do seek unbiased advice on your situation, for example from a hotline or charity for young people.

* Don't sleep on the streets, stay with someone you know.

* Don't act on impulse – for example after a huge row, or if you are upset.

Groups at risk of becoming homeless

One thing is clear. Poorer people are much more at risk of homelessness than better-off people. When someone is wealthy or has a regular job with a good salary, they are in a better position to buy or rent a home. People without money or a job are much less likely to be able to afford a proper home. Their chances of getting a mortgage are low. If they are lucky, they may find a good place to rent or they may qualify for social housing.

However, many people end up renting whatever space they can find and afford. If they fall ill, suffer an injury, lose their job or cannot pay their rent on time, they may be evicted. Most people do find another place to live, but some become homeless.

Who is at risk?

Although poor people are much more at risk of homelessness, homeless individuals come from many different backgrounds and do not easily fit in to one group. People of all ages – women, men, boys and girls – can become homeless.

Sleeping on the streets in all weathers means that blankets and sleeping bags quickly become damp and dirty.

In some respects, men seem more likely to become homeless than women. Men are more likely to be heavy drinkers, drug users and gamblers, so are more at risk of homelessness through addiction or mental health problems.

One group especially at risk is that of former soldiers. Some have been traumatized by their experiences and are in poor health, others are unable to adapt to life outside the military or find a suitable job (see page 31).

A survey in the USA found that 40% of homeless men had been in the armed forces, like the man in the picture above. Many of these homeless men had served in wars in Vietnam and Iraq.

Another group at risk are immigrants and refugees. Many arrive in a new city or country and find shelter with friends from their own community. Others come without any connections. In the worst cases, they can find themselves living on the streets. For example, the *Guardian* reported in 2004 that a 47-year-old man was found dead in a dingy, smelly rubbish room below a top London restaurant. He had been secretly living in a tiny alcove behind rubbish skips, which he had boarded up with pieces of cardboard. He was an immigrant from the Ukraine and had been working as a kitchen porter.

It happened to me

'I'm an outreach worker. I go out on the streets, talk to homeless young people. They don't realize how vulnerable they are. I want to reach them before the drug dealers. I try to help them, find them a safe place to stay, maybe contact their family. It's hard work and not always successful.'

Kim, homeless support worker.

This young mother and child have nowhere to live and are sitting with their possessions in a doorway in Jackson, Mississippi, USA.

Women and children

Some women and children can lose their homes when families separate, especially when a women leaves an abusive relationship. She and her children may be victims of violence, or threatened with violence. The woman may be fleeing in fear of her life with nowhere to turn. She may not have friends to shelter her, and she may not have money for a room. Some find shelter in special refuges; others end up on the streets.

The numbers can be high. For example, in the USA a survey of homeless mothers in 2003 found a quarter of the women had been recent victims of domestic violence. In the UK, a survey of homeless women aged 30–49 found that 63% listed domestic violence as the main reason they had become homeless.

Family breakdown

Family breakdowns are not always about violence. They can also be caused by stress, overcrowding, financial worries and bad personal relationships. In the past, extended families were often willing to help out but today this is less common. In England, in 2005, 38% of households were homeless because friends or relatives were no longer willing to offer housing.

TALK ABOUT

Think about the groups most at danger of becoming homeless and the reasons why that might be.

✳ **What do you think are the main causes of homelessness?**

✳ **Are there ways we can act to help people at risk?**

For ideas on how to extend Talk About discussions please see the Notes for Teachers on page 47.

Some people become homeless not just because they are poor but because they lack social networks – family, friends, workmates – and contacts with groups who can help, such as government agencies, charities and religious groups. They feel isolated and alone. Becoming homeless cuts them off from mainstream society and makes them feel even more helpless.

Despite their problems, most people do not become homeless. Somehow, often with the help of family, friends and charitable organizations, they find their way into permanent housing and a better life. Those who do become homeless often have a long journey into destitution and isolation, lurching from one crisis to another – money problems, abuse, addiction, bad health, mental illness or family breakdown.

Once someone becomes homeless, his or her problems multiply. Their lives become even more chaotic. Housing organizations say that although it may take a long time for a person to become homeless, once they have lived on the streets for a month or more, street life becomes the norm and it is much more difficult for them to move back into mainstream society.

Many homeless families seek help with housing from government authorities and charities. Sometimes the only option is a homeless shelter, but life there can be noisy, dirty and unsafe.

Chapter 3

Homelessness and children

Homelessness has a devastating effect on young people, blighting their lives and opportunities for the future. Some young people live on the streets. However, most homeless children live with their families in shared or temporary housing and are not registered as homeless or counted in the numbers of the homeless.

In poor countries, there are large numbers of homeless children living on the streets. Some maintain links with their family and others live in gangs. Many survive by begging, stealing or doing small amounts of work, such as carrying shopping or washing cars. The United Nations (UN) agency, Habitat, says that there may be over 100 million street children, mainly in Asia, Africa and Latin America.

Runaways at risk

In richer countries, the numbers of street children are much smaller. Many are runaways or 'throwaways'. In a survey of young people staying in homeless shelters in several US cities, half told interviewers that their parents had told them to leave or knew that they were leaving and did not care. In another study, almost half said that they had been physically abused. Others had been in care and become homeless when their foster places finished.

A survey in England found that around 10% of children under 16 years of age had run away from home at least once. Most had been away only one or two nights, and stayed with relatives and friends before returning home.

A homeless teenager with her dog on the streets of London. The dog is more than a pet – it provides her with warmth on the cold nights and helps protect her.

There are millions of street children in Brazil. Most live in gangs in the large cities, like this group in São Paulo. They have fun together but they also face great danger.

In the media

The housing charity, Shelter, claims that one in seven children is growing up homeless or in 'bad' housing. Shelter says 1.6 million youngsters in Britain are living in housing judged to be temporary, unfit or overcrowded. The charity, which is marking its fortieth anniversary, described the situation as a 'scandal.'

Family problems

Some of the runaway children said that they had been pushed out by uncaring or abusive parents or step-parents, many of whom had drug or alcohol problems. Many said that they were unhappy at school, had been excluded from classes or had been in trouble with the police. Most at risk were the poorest children from unstable families and 'looked after' children who had been in children's homes or foster homes.

Often runaways find themselves in greater danger on the streets than they were in at home. Some are taken in by abusive or controlling adults. Once a young person starts sleeping rough, they have to defend themselves against tougher adults. They are more likely to turn to drink or drugs, or to become involved with crime or sex work.

Homeless children and families

Most homeless children are not runaways. They live with their families, sharing with relatives or staying in temporary housing, such as hotels and hostels, hoping that one day they will have a proper home. Homeless children come from different backgrounds, but what they have in common is that their families cannot afford to rent or buy a home of their own.

Homeless children are often found to live in crowded and poor-quality housing. They have a roof over their head but they must share their rooms – and sometimes beds – with family members. Temporary housing can be poor-quality, noisy and dirty, and is often situated in the worst areas. This causes illness and children's mental health suffers because of the constant strain and insecurity. Being homeless and poor places extra strains on family life. Quarrels can lead to family breakdown.

Many homeless children live with their families in unsuitable and overcrowded housing. Here a family in London's East End share a room, with several of them sleeping in the same bed.

Education

Schooling is another problem. It is not easy to do well in your studies if you are constantly moving schools or have no quiet space to work. This has consequences in later life because children lack the qualifications they need to get a good job.

A homeless runaway called Chris says: *'They call me a sofa surfer. It sounds fun but it isn't. I left home a few months ago after another row with my step-father. I just couldn't take it any more. I stay with friends now – sleeping on the floor or on a sofa. I move around a lot. I want to go to college but it's hard to focus.'*

TALK ABOUT

* How can we help children who have run away from home?
* Should they return home, be placed into foster care or given other housing (like a hostel)?

Chapter 4
Addiction and homelessness

An addict is a person who has a craving for substances such as alcohol or drugs. They need to use them more and more frequently to satisfy their habit and finally they become totally dependent on them. Their addiction becomes more important than anything else in their lives, including their home and family.

One of the most common ideas about homeless people is that most of them are addicted to either alcohol or drugs. In fact, this is not true. Most homeless people are not substance abusers and most drug and alcohol addicts are not homeless. However, addiction is more common among certain types of homeless people, especially rough sleepers.

The relationship between addiction and homelessness is complex. Do people become homeless because they are addicted to drugs or alcohol, or do they become addicted because they are homeless? Being poor, in an abusive relationship, living in an area where drug dealing is common – all these factors make people more at risk of becoming both addicted and homeless. Well-off people can also become addicted, and in some cases this can lead to them losing their homes and families.

Street drinkers may see drinking alcohol in a public place as a harmless social activity but others can find it distressing and anti-social.

Addiction can begin at an early age. For these children in Nepal, South Asia, drinking alcohol keeps out the cold on freezing nights and helps them forget their situation.

Addiction on the streets

Crisis, a UK charity, says that 81% of the homeless people it encountered on the streets or in shelters were addicted either to drugs (usually heroin) or alcohol, and 67% said that the addiction was a major reason for becoming homeless. Once they were on the streets, many had started using new drugs. Many shelters and hostels will not allow alcohol or drugs on their premises, so addicts find themselves staying on the streets.

Once a person is on the streets, it becomes tempting to find comfort in drugs or drink. Alcohol helps people to endure the long nights in the cold and rain, desperately trying to keep warm. If they are ill, drink and drugs provide a form of self-medication, which makes them feel better – at least for a time.

It happened to me

'I got into drugs because everyone else was doing them. If someone offered me rehab [rehabilitation] I'd take it. If you gave me a flat with a TV and a fridge I would sell them to feed my habit. If I was given rehab and then accommodation and then a job maybe it would be different.'

Tony, homeless drug addict.

Homeless drug addicts often share needles, putting themselves at risk of infection. Used needles can infect others, including children who find them thrown away in parks.

Drink and drugs

Drinking is often a social activity. Groups of street drinkers, mainly men, gather in streets, parks and public places. Generally they drink the cheapest and strongest drinks they can find, to give them the buzz they seek. Some beg for spare change, or shout and swear at passers-by, although most are not violent. Their presence frightens people and they may be arrested or moved on by police.

Drugs tend to be less visible than alcohol, at least to outsiders. Drugs such as heroin or crack cocaine can be deadly. It is not simply the effect of the drugs that is dangerous, but the conditions in which they are used. Injecting drugs with dirty (unsterilized) needles spreads diseases such as HIV/AIDS and hepatitis (chronic liver infection). Many young drug users, boys as well as girls, sell their bodies for sex to earn money for drugs.

TALK ABOUT

Consider the statements below. Do you agree or disagree with them?

✲ **All homeless people have a problem with drugs or alcohol.**

✲ **People can only overcome addiction if they help themselves.**

✲ **People who drink heavily or take drugs should be left alone to manage their own lives.**

✲ **It is wrong to spend money trying to help people overcome addiction.**

✲ **We should not give housing to people with addictions because they do not appreciate it.**

Overcoming addiction

Can people overcome their addictions? Yes, many can and do, if and when they get the right help and support. However, treatment and rehabilitation programmes are intensive and expensive. Often the addict has to attend regular meetings or go into a residential treatment centre like a hospital and take medicines or drug substitutes. Most people would find this difficult, but it is even harder for destitute homeless people, whose lives are already chaotic.

One of the biggest problems is that there are far more addicts needing treatment than places available. So there are long waiting lists. Inevitably, homeless people, with all their other problems, are at the bottom of the list. If a former addict is given permanent housing, it provides a stable base to rebuild their lives. However, it is easy to relapse if life seems boring and meaningless, so finding a new interest in life – such as a job – can be a crucial factor in overcoming addiction.

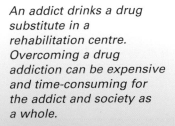

An addict drinks a drug substitute in a rehabilitation centre. Overcoming a drug addiction can be expensive and time-consuming for the addict and society as a whole.

Chapter 5

Staying clean and healthy

It can be hard to stay healthy if you are homeless. Staying in poor-quality, temporary housing or on the streets, eating poorly and living with stress all have a negative effect on health. Homeless people find it harder to get health care than almost any other group in society.

Sometimes it is poor health that pushes people into homelessness. Severe illness or serious injury can mean that people are off work for weeks or months. Without a regular pay cheque from a job, a worker may fall behind with their rent or mortgage. As a result, the family must seek cheaper housing. In the worst cases, they may end up on the streets.

Keeping yourself and your clothes clean is difficult if you are homeless. There are few opportunities for washing and drying clothes. This homeless woman is in Karachi, Pakistan.

Health on the streets

For rough sleepers, life outside may not seem so bad during the hot summer months but it gets much tougher in the winter. Sleeping on wet cardboard in doorways or huddled by heating vents means that people are constantly cold and wet, and sleeping bags and blankets quickly become damp and dirty.

A homeless girl in Brazil drinks from a container of milk she found while searching through rubbish.

Not surprisingly, rough sleepers often develop colds and become infested by lice or bitten by rats. In England, rough sleepers are three times as likely as housed people to have chronic chest and breathing problems. Frostbite, leg ulcers and trench-foot, caused by constant cold and damp, can affect them. Street violence and moving vehicles also cause injuries.

Most rough sleepers do not eat regularly or healthily. Instead, they buy fast food because it is cheap, or they eat leftovers from café tables and rubbish bins. If they are lucky they may have a filling meal at a charity soup kitchen. Living and sleeping on the streets makes people age quickly. Death can come sooner than for people who have a home to live in.

It happened to me

'I was 16 when I got a place in a hostel but it was terrible. There were hundreds of people there – and the way some of the older men looked at me made me shiver. It was filthy – there were cockroaches and the toilets were disgusting. You couldn't cook there, so I lived on sandwiches – I lost loads of weight and ended up getting really ill.'

Dominque, London.

This homeless man in Russia is provided with a hot meal, clean clothes and a roof over his head. But tomorrow he will face another tough day on the streets.

In the
media

Refuse collectors rescued a homeless Polish man from a rubbish truck after hearing his cries for help. The man had spent the night in a rubbish container in Arnoldstein in southern Austria. One of the workers heard his cries and stopped the machine just as it was about to start squashing the rubbish.

Temporary housing

It is not just street people who suffer. Homeless people in temporary accommodation, such as hostels, shelters and squats, also fare badly. Although they have a roof over their heads, their accommodation is often poor quality. It may consist of short-life housing (homes due for demolition or refurbishment), or high-rise flats with no space to play.

Homeless children

In 2002, the housing charity Shelter estimated that 750,000 children in England were living in damp, run-down housing. As a result, the children were more likely to suffer from medical conditions like gastroenteritis and asthma. In the USA, the National Coalition for the Homeless says that homeless children experience poor health twice as often as other children and have high rates of asthma, ear infections, stomach problems and speech problems. They do not walk or talk as early as other children.

Health care

Although homeless people are less healthy than the general population, it is much more difficult for them to find good health care. Even in countries with free health care, like Britain or Denmark, it can be hard for people in temporary housing to find a regular doctor or health centre. When there is a sudden illness or accident, people use emergency services, but often they arrive too late for prevention or cure. In countries where health care is not free or is restricted, homeless people have even more difficulties staying healthy.

Health centres and hospitals may not know how to help people on the streets. Rough sleepers often dislike and distrust health workers who they see as figures of authority. There are often special health services for homeless people, sometimes run by charities or religious organizations. They have special expertise to deal with the most common conditions that affect homeless people, and do not ask too many questions about their lives.

Chapter 6

Mental health

A homeless woman spends her days pushing her possessions in a home-made trolley on the streets of New York City, USA.

All over the world, homeless people seem to use the same words over and over. They say how worried and anxious they are, how insecure they feel, how it is so difficult to think ahead and plan for the future. They feel that they do not belong to the wider community – that they belong nowhere.

People living on the streets or in homeless shelters say that they do not feel safe and fear being attacked. People in temporary accommodation worry when, or whether, they will find a proper home. Overcrowding can lead to arguments and violence. Rather than providing a safe haven, home can be a battleground, with no escape.

Mental illnesses

Mental health refers to a person's emotional, spiritual and psychological well-being. When people are living well and feel secure, they are less stressed and worried. People who lead insecure and anxious lives, including homeless people, are more likely to have mental health problems.

The most common problem is depression, where a person feels constantly sad and upset. The depression may be so acute that the person cannot work or care for themselves. Other types of mental illness lead people to become delusional or paranoid, hearing voices or believing they are being pursued by real or imagined people. Sometimes they become violent, turning against themselves or others; sometimes they are silent and withdrawn.

The links between homelessness and mental health are complicated. People who are homeless are more likely to have mental health problems but, in turn, some people become homeless because they are mentally ill. They may leave home because they are delusional or paranoid, fearing their lives are at risk if they stay, or they

For homeless people, sympathetic human contact is vital to remaining connected with the outside world.

may just drift away because they are depressed and unhappy. Their illness may cause them to lose their job, their income and their home. If they are a danger to themselves or others, they may have been asked or ordered to leave home. Whatever the case, when a person is mentally ill and homeless, their situation becomes much worse.

DOs & DON'Ts

If you are feeling depressed or suicidal:

* Do try to stay calm and keep in touch with friends and family – things will improve if you can talk about your problems.

* Don't bottle up your feelings and thoughts. Talk to someone you trust and seek help.

* Don't act on impulse. It is easy to do the wrong thing when you are depressed or upset.

* Don't turn to alcohol or drugs. Although they may make you feel better temporarily, they will make things much worse if you become addicted.

Rough sleepers and mental health

In the UK, people sleeping rough are eleven times more likely to have mental health problems and people living in hostels are eight times more likely to have mental health problems than the general population. One of the most tragic consequences is the high suicide rate. Crisis, a homelessness charity, found that rough sleepers in England were thirty-five times more likely to commit suicide than the general population and that one third of young homeless people had attempted suicide.

Mental health services and the homeless

It can be difficult for a homeless person to find the help they need. They may be ashamed to admit their problems or unwilling to seek treatment, especially if they have had bad experiences, and many fear prejudice and stigma.

Rough sleepers seem to fare the worst. Few have access to a regular doctor or clinic and many do not trust health services. In addition, many people have bad health, drink alcohol or take drugs, making effective treatment much harder. There are few facilities to meet their requirements, for example their need for rest and a peaceful place away from the rough streets or overcrowded hostels. Even when they are rehoused, they may face eviction, because they act in ways that are violent or anti-social or they do not have the support they need to cope.

Many homeless people are ignored by everyone. This makes them even more inward-looking and isolated. This photo shows a homeless person in Milan, Italy.

Alex, a homeless former soldier, remembers: *'I was sleeping rough on the streets. I became very inward-looking and wary of people. I managed to get myself to an ex-service hostel, where my mental illness was diagnosed and treated. I'm OK now and looking for a job.'*

A hostel can offer shelter but not privacy, as dozens of people share a room. Some hostels give special support to those with mental health problems.

TALK ABOUT

✳ **If you were at risk of being homeless, how would you feel?**

✳ **Where do you think you could turn for help?**

Chapter 7

Working and earning

It is difficult to find work without a stable and secure place to call home. People in temporary accommodation often find themselves housed in the poorest areas, where jobs are few and insecure, and pay is low. Even when jobs are available, there are other problems facing homeless people.

Homeless people tend to be poor, with few educational qualifications and skills. They are less likely to have strong family or community ties and they may lack the confidence and persistence needed to find and keep a job. The situation may be getting worse. When the homeless charity, St Mungo's in London, UK, interviewed 100 homeless people in 1986, it found that 83% had some form of paid employment. A similar survey in 2005 found only 5% in paid employment.

Many homeless people lead unstable lives, moving from place to place. Without a permanent address, they cannot obtain the documents they need to apply for work (such as a national insurance or social security number). Also, people with jobs usually need to keep regular hours and homeless people are unlikely to be able to do this.

A woman sleeps in a homeless shelter in New York City, USA. Without a permanent address, it can be difficult to find and keep a job.

Nevertheless, many homeless people do hold down jobs, often working long hours for low pay. But even when people earn a good wage, housing costs may be too high for them to move into good-quality, permanent homes. Instead they are trapped – as they work, they are not given priority for the social housing schemes that poorer or unemployed people might benefit from.

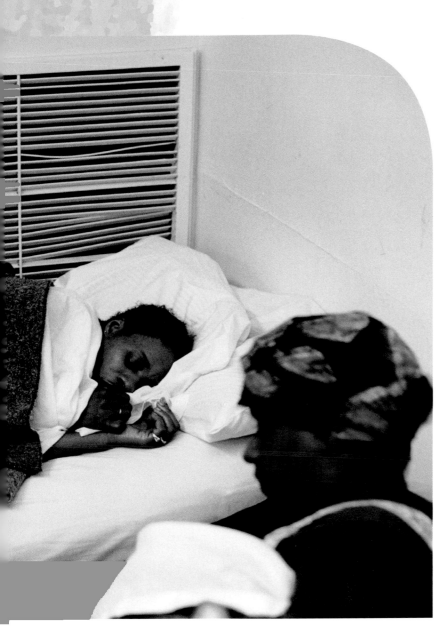

Homeless people say that employers' attitudes are one of their biggest barriers to finding work. Employers usually see homeless people as untrustworthy and unreliable and few are willing to offer a homeless person a chance for employment. Many employers associate homeless people with the hardened beggars they see on the streets, rather than people who need help to overcome their problems.

It happened to me

'I volunteer with a small charity. My organization really trusts me. They let me take all the money to the bank at the end of the day. But I don't talk about my housing situation. I am scared that if they knew that I lived in a hostel that they would think that I might steal the money or spend it on drugs.'

Lizzie, Birmingham, UK.

Jobs versus benefits

Not all homeless people are in a position to take paid work. They may be mentally or physically ill or disabled, or addicted to alcohol or drugs. They may be caring for young children or a sick partner.

In richer countries, many homeless people receive social security benefits or welfare, which are supposed to pay for basic living costs – housing, food and drink, toiletries, and utilities, like electricity and heating. Life on benefits can be hard. It is a constant struggle to juggle everyday costs with paying rent and bills while trying to save for special occasions. However, benefits are relatively secure and are paid regularly. For homeless people, taking a job, especially a low-paid job, can be a gamble. They may find themselves worse off in work, as benefits can be reduced or taken away once they get a job.

Two homeless men try to raise funds through a combination of music and an appeal to public sympathy.

It happened to me

'I work full time, earn a decent wage, but it's not enough to rent privately. My son and I live in a one-room temporary flat. There is one heater and it's freezing. The guilt and pain you feel is overwhelming. It's not right to treat people like this, when most are trying to earn a decent living and raise their kids. It has to stop.'

Becky, London, UK.

The Big Issue Foundation aims to help homeless people earn money by selling magazines. This man sells the Big Issue in Osaka, Japan.

Young people

For homeless young people, the financial situation is terrifying. Few qualify for benefits and many are too young to work legally. For those able to work, well-paid jobs are hard to come by, especially if they have no qualifications. Even if they can find a job, they may not have the physical, mental or emotional strength to keep it for long.

It is not surprising that some young people resort to begging or shoplifting or other illegal activities. Some become buskers and others sell street newspapers, such as the *Big Issue* or *Street Times*. Many say that they do not want to do these things but they have no option – there is no other way they can survive.

In the developing world, the situation is different. Homeless children often pick up unskilled jobs – carrying shopping or collecting rubbish – often working in gangs. These jobs do not bring in regular income and nearly everything is spent on basics, like food.

Beggars are often found in societies where there are wide gaps between the richest and the poorest people. These young beggars are on the streets of China.

Begging on the streets

'Why don't they get a job, rather than begging? Then they could find somewhere to live.' You might have heard people say this as they pass a beggar on the street. You may have said this yourself.

Take another look at the beggar. Probably they look cold and dirty, with lank, unwashed hair and badly fitting, ill-assorted clothes. Some may look confused, others may have been drinking. Many refuse to make eye contact – perhaps they are ashamed or frightened. They might hold a sign saying 'Hungry and homeless', or they may just have a cup or piece of cardboard with a few coins scattered around.

A survey of street beggars and street drinkers in the UK by the charity Crisis found some surprising results. Only a few of them were full-time beggars. Many were on benefits and others supplemented their income by selling street newspapers, by busking or by shoplifting. About half were sleeping rough, others were in hostels or staying with friends, and a few had permanent homes.

Many people in the survey had been on the streets for years and about half had a serious health problem or an alcohol or drug addiction. Most said that they started begging to get money for alcohol or drugs.

Begging is a controversial subject. Many people give money to beggars in the belief that personal charity is good in itself and that beggars will spend the money they are given on food or a bed for the night. Critics say that most of the proceeds go on alcohol or drugs. Instead, they say that it would be better if people gave money to homelessness charities working for long-term solutions. Beggars themselves often defend their actions by saying that if they did not beg they would have to steal or shoplift to survive.

Young homeless people can be found on the streets in rich countries. Some have run away from abusive families and have nowhere else to go.

TALK ABOUT

✳ **Do you think it is right to give money to beggars?**

✳ **What other ways do you think you can help?**

Chapter 8

Helping the homeless

How can society help homeless people? The most straightforward answer is by ensuring that there is enough housing available for everyone who needs it. However, homelessness is a social as well as a physical problem. Putting an end to it is also about helping individuals to take the steps that help them out of their homeless situation.

Building more homes

An obvious solution to the problem of homelessness is to increase the number of homes available. But this is a difficult process as it means building new homes and renovating older ones. It involves getting planning permission, buying land and building supplies, organizing builders, and connecting utilities such as water and electricity. As all these tasks can take years, the building of more homes is a long-term solution.

However, it is not enough to just have more homes. They need to be affordable homes for the poorest groups, who are most likely to be homeless. This usually means social housing, where rents are lower than in the private sector. The demand for social housing is always greater than the supply.

It happened to me

'My rent has increased by $165 [approximately £83] a month in the last year. As homeowners lose their homes and move their families into apartments, the landlords here excitedly talk about the current "boom" in their business – they don't think what that really means for their own future, let alone the futures of their fellow citizens and neighbours.'

Ben, Austin, Texas, USA.

Many governments say that social housing should go to families with children, rather than single people. People with convictions for drink or drug abuse or anti-social behaviour are often excluded from social housing. This means that many homeless people miss out, although they are in genuine need.

Governments often encourage people to buy their own homes. However, many people are too poor to borrow through a mortgage, while others find themselves paying a large proportion of their income in repayments and interest. If interest rates rise, people may no longer be able to afford these payments. In the worst cases, people may end up losing their home. For example, starting in 2006 many households in the USA found that rising interest rates meant that they could no longer pay their mortgages. Many hurriedly tried to sell their homes, only to find that house prices were falling. Although most people in this situation will turn to renting, some will become homeless.

This boy lives in a social housing project in Dublin, Ireland. Not all social housing offers children a place to play.

Helping homeless people

What is the best way to help homeless people? There are no easy answers because, as we have seen, homeless people are individuals with different problems and circumstances. The most simple group are people who just need a helping hand to get into proper housing. Once they have been rehoused, they can start to sort out any other problems they may have, such as jobs, schooling or family issues.

Many homeless people have complex problems, such as drug or alcohol addiction, physical or mental illness, and family and emotional difficulties. Homelessness is only one of the many problems they face. In some cases it is a consequence, rather than a cause, of their problems. Experience shows that it is not enough to give these people a home. They need extra support to help them solve some of the problems that caused them to become homeless in the first place.

There is a huge demand for social housing, especially in big cities. These public housing apartment blocks are on the Lower East Side of New York City, USA.

FACTS

HOMELESSNESS IN THE USA

✳ **Every night around 750,000 people in the USA sleep in a homeless shelter or on the streets.**

✳ **One third are families with children, one quarter are disabled and one third are black.**

Source: US government figures, March 2007.

Practical help

Going from homeless to being housed is a big step. Some homelessness organizations say that the best way is to take it step by step – first by talking to a homeless person, then by giving practical help such as food, then a bed in a hostel or shelter and then by encouraging them to move into permanent housing. Even then there are likely to be obstacles. Long-term homeless people often do not understand how to deal with the basics of everyday living, such as cooking a meal, cleaning, and paying bills on time. They need help to finish their education or find and keep a job. Some need specialist help to overcome an addiction – and extra help to pick them up if they relapse.

Many charities help homeless people. Here, young volunteers distribute food, drink and blankets to people on the streets.

Campaigning for change

For a few people, homelessness is like a revolving door, which they enter and exit regularly. Given a home of their own, they feel lonely and trapped. They have become used to life on the streets. They prefer the buzz of street life and their friendships with other rough sleepers. These people usually turn down offers of housing, until they are old or ill, by which time it may be too late to change their lives.

Homeless people enjoy a hot Christmas dinner served by volunteers at Los Angeles Mission. Holidays can be a tough and lonely time for street people.

A nun feeds a baby in the Shishu Bhavan orphanage, founded by Mother Theresa in Calcutta, India. The orphanage cares for 300 children, some disabled and abandoned on the city streets.

In the
media

All over the world, there are organizations that speak out against homelessness. Some campaign to prevent homelessness, arguing for more houses or lower rents or fairer treatment of people at risk. Other organizations help support homeless people by providing soup and sandwiches, running hostels for young runaways or long-term homeless people, organizing medical care, training or jobs, helping addicts to overcome addiction – and much more.

Steve Williamson received an anonymous flyer in his mailbox last month. It said a four-story apartment complex for mentally ill homeless people was being built in his neighbourhood in Seattle. Williamson knew he had to do something. His father had committed suicide after a struggle with mental illness. Williamson had recently vowed to speak out against stigmas and stereotypes about the mentally ill. So instead of joining opponents who worry that the project will make their streets less safe, Williamson and several dozen neighbours formed a group to welcome the project.

This picture shows a scene at the 2007 Homeless World Cup in Copenhagen, Denmark. Over fifty countries entered teams in the competition.

Tackling the problem

Organizations made up of homeless people are new developments. Many are in poorer countries or in countries where there is a big division between rich and poor, such as India or South Africa, where millions of people live in slums and shanty towns or on the streets. Other groups are in richer countries, where homelessness is less common but still devastating for individuals and for society as a whole.

One such organization formed by the homeless is 'The Homeless World Cup,' an international soccer tournament which brings together homeless people to play football, learn new skills and raise self-esteem. Over three-quarters of those who participated in the 2006 tournament in South Africa said that taking part encouraged them to change their lives. The 2007 tournament in Denmark saw Scotland beat Poland in the final by 9 goals to 3 in front of packed crowds in the city hall square.

In the media

'I'm extremely pleased that Copenhagen will host the 2007 Homeless World Cup. The tournament focuses our attention on homelessness and gives Copenhageners an opportunity to see homeless people as real people who have goals and resources, just like everybody else. I hope that we can help to break down prejudices.'

Mikkel Warming, Mayor of Copenhagen, Denmark, 2007.

✳ Can you think of five ways we could provide help to homeless people?

✳ Are there any ways that you can think of to encourage schools and young people to get involved in helping the homeless?

The captain of Poland's team, Rafal Rozonski, said, *'One of my strongest dreams has been realized: to represent my country and participate in the World Cup final. We are good fighters. It can be very hard to be homeless but playing soccer makes you forget about that. You can be free.'*

Homeless people themselves often say that one of their biggest problems is the discrimination and stigma they face from wider society. They acknowledge that they may have problems but say that society does not understand the stresses they face. Most want to go back to having a stable life. They say that in many respects they are like other people, but just need that extra help to become full-serving members of society.

'We want a proper home!' Homeless people in New York City demonstrate for homes and human rights.

Glossary

benefits Payments by the government to add to people's income, usually paid to people who are unemployed, ill, disabled or with young children. (In the USA, benefits are called 'welfare').

busker A person who sings or plays music on the street for money.

chronic Constant, something that occurs again and again.

delusional A false belief or impression, often a sign of mental illness.

derelict Very run down.

destitute Without possessions, in extreme poverty.

eviction Expulsion from a house or flat.

gastroenteritis An infection of the guts, caused by viruses, bacteria or other germs. It causes stomach pains, vomiting and diarrhoea.

HIV/AIDS A deadly illness, usually resulting from unsafe sex or using dirty needles.

hostel A place providing temporary shelter to homeless people, also called a homeless shelter. Shelters can provide temporary homes.

housing market Overall numbers and types of houses for sale or rent.

interest The cost of borrowing money.

mortgage A special long-term loan to buy a house or flat.

not-for-profit organization An organization, like a charity or religious organization, that exists to support poor or vulnerable people or provide services, rather than to sell goods or make a profit.

paranoid A deep fear or distrust of other people.

relapse Return to a former state, usually refers to addiction to drink or drugs.

Safe haven A place where someone feels safe and protected.

shanty towns Areas of poor and makeshift housing on the outskirts of a city.

slum Rundown city area with overcrowded and bad housing.

social housing Housing owned by government or not-for-profit organizations and rented to tenants.

sofa surfer Term given to a person without a permanent home, sleeping in other people's homes, often on a sofa or the floor.

squatting Living in a building for free, with or without permission.

stereotype A particular (often inaccurate) idea.

stigma A shameful feeling.

tenant A person who rents a house or flat.

traumatized Emotional shock with a long-lasting effect.

UN An international organization that acts to ensure human rights are protected and that countries follow international laws.

Further information

Notes for Teachers:

The Talk About panels are to be used to encourage debate and avoid the polarization of views. One way of doing this is to use 'continuum lines'. Think of a range of statements or opinions about the topics that can then be considered by the pupils. An imaginary line is constructed that pupils can stand along to show what they feel in response to each statement (please see above). If they strongly agree or disagree with the viewpoint they can stand by the signs, if the response is somewhere in between they stand along the line in the relevant place. If the response is 'neither agree, nor disagree' or they 'don't know' then they stand at an equal distance from each sign, in the middle. Alternatively, continuum lines can be drawn out on paper and pupils can mark a cross on the line to reflect their views.

Books to read

What if We Do Nothing? Poverty by Cath Senker (Franklin Watts, 2007)

It Happened to Me: Runaway by A. Neustatter (Franklin Watts, 2007)

Why do people live on the streets? by Kaye Stearman (Wayland, 2000)

Websites and helplines

Big Issue Foundation

An international organization working with homeless people in the UK, Australia, Japan, South Africa and Namibia.

Website: www.bigissue.com
Contact: contact@bigissue.com

Crisis

Housing advice and support, especially for single people and rough sleepers.

Website: www.crisis.org.uk
Contact: enquiries@crisis.org.uk

European Federation of National Organizations working with the Homeless

Information on homelessness in 30 European countries.
Website: www.feantsa.org
Contact: office@feantsa.org

Homeless International

UK charity that supports community-led housing and services with partner organizations in cities in Asia and Africa.

Website: www.homeless-international.org
Contact: info@homeless-international.org

Homelessness World Cup

Information about the project and tournaments.
Website: www2.homelessness worldcup.org
Contact: info@homelessness worldcup.org

Homelessness Link

Information about services for homeless people in the UK.

Website: www.homeless.org.uk
Contact: info@homelesslink.org.uk

National Coalition for the Homeless

US organization of individuals and organizations working against homelessness.
Website: www.nationalhomeless.org

Shelter

Housing advice for all regions of the UK.
Website: www.shelter.org.uk
Contact: info@shelter.org.uk
Phone: 00 44 (0)808 800 4444 (Free 24-hour helpline)

St Mungo's

Projects rehousing rough sleepers in London.
Website: www.stmungos.org.uk
Contact: info@mungos.org

UN Habitat – United Nations Human Settlements Programme

Information on housing and homelessness worldwide.
Website: www.habitat.org

Index

Entries in **bold** are for pictures.

TALK ABOUT

Contents of titles in the series:

Bullying

978 0 7502 4617 0
1. Let's talk about bullying
2. What is bullying?
3. How does it feel to be bullied?
4. Who gets bullied?
5. Why do people bully?
6. Beating bullying
7. Bullying in society

Eating Disorders and Body Image

978 0 7502 4936 2
1. What are eating disorders?
2. Food and the body
3. What does it mean to have an eating disorder?
4. Who gets eating disorders?
5. What causes eating disorders?
6. Preventing problems
7. The treatment of eating disorders

Racism

978 0 7502 4935 5
1. What is racism?
2. Why are people racist?
3. What do racists do?
4. Hidden racism
5. What is religious prejudice?
6. Racism against migrants
7. Nazi racial policies
8. What can we do about racism?

Drugs

978 0 7502 4937 9
1. What are drugs?
2. Why do we take drugs?
3. What about drinking and smoking?
4. What's the law on drugs?
5. What about cannabis?
6. What other drugs are there?
7. Paying the price
8. It's your choice

Homelessness

978 0 7502 4934 8
1. What is homelessness?
2. Why do people become homeless?
3. Homelessness and children
4. Addiction and homelessness
5. Staying clean and healthy
6. Mental health
7. Working and earning
8. Helping the homeless

Youth Crime

978 0 7502 4938 6
1. What is crime?
2. Crime past and present
3. Why does youth crime happen?
4. Behaving badly
5. Crimes of theft
6. Crimes of violence
7. What happens if you commit a crime?
8. What can you do about crime?

WAYLAND